W9-DDK-735

Chocolate Dessert in Crème Anglaise, page 66

Prosciutto-and-Fontina Panini, page 42

FRASIER™

Café Nervosa™

THE CONNOISSEUR'S COOKBOOK

Oxmoor
House®

Published by Oxmoor House, Inc.
Book Division of Southern Progress Corporation
P.O. Box 2463, Birmingham, Alabama 35201
© 1996 by Paramount Pictures Corporation

Recipes and food photography © 1996 by Oxmoor House, Inc.
FRASIER™ Text and Photography © 1996 Paramount Pictures Corporation
Book introduction by Anne Flett-Giordano, Supervising Producer FRASIER™
Oxmoor House Authorized User.

Library of Congress Catalog Number: 96-69578
ISBN: 0-8487-1550-0
Manufactured in the United States of America
First Printing 1996

Editor-in-Chief: Nancy Fitzpatrick Wyatt
Senior Foods Editor: Susan Carlisle Payne
Senior Editor, Editorial Services: Olivia Kindig Wells
Art Director: James Boone

FRASIER™ Café Nervosa™ THE CONNOISSEUR'S COOKBOOK

Editor: Julie Fisher
Copy Editor: Jacqueline B. Giovanelli
Editorial Assistant: Stacey Geary
Designer: Clare T. Minges
Production and Distribution Director: Phillip Lee
Associate Production Manager: Vanessa Cobbs Richardson
Production Assistant: Valerie L. Heard
Project Manager: Teresa Wilson Lux
Photography by Ralph Anderson, Jim Bathie, Tina Evans, Lee Isaacs, Howard L. Puckett, and
    Charles Walton IV
Photostyling by Cindy Manning Barr, Kay E. Clarke, Virginia R. Cravens, and Cathy Muir
Back Cover: Coffee-Toffee Parfait (page 82)

To order more copies of FRASIER™ Café Nervosa™ THE CONNOISSEUR'S COOKBOOK, write to
Oxmoor House, P.O. Box 2463, Birmingham, AL 35201.

CONTENTS

Introduction

FRASIER:

Frasier Crane writing a cookbook . . . whatever possessed him?

NILES:

Perhaps his insatiable need to feed his big, fat ego.

FRASIER:

Oh, very nice, Niles.

NILES:

Well, one can't help but notice how deftly you managed to work your name into the opening sentence while omitting any mention of your co-author. Who, I might add, should rightfully get first billing since he did most of the typing while you did most of the sampling.

FRASIER:

I was just getting to you.

NILES:

Hurry.

FRASIER:

Recently, while enjoying our daily repast at Café Nervosa, *Niles* and I posed the question, "What have food and drink to do with psychology?" The answer was elementary: everything. A simple cup of coffee — a grande nonfat, half-caf latte with a soupçon of nutmeg, for example — has the power to transport one's spirits. Conversely, I've seen grown men reduced to tears over a broken cappuccino machine.

NILES:

You can hardly blame me. Maris's opera group was performing Wagner. You try staring down a double-barreled evening of aging society women wearing braids and breastplates and caterwauling in German without a fortifying shot of caffeine.

FRASIER:

As I was saying . . . Emotions and food go together like New Wives and Old Money. When we're depressed, we eat to cheer up. When we're nervous, we eat to calm down. When we're alone, well, to quote Robert Morley, "No man is lonely while eating spaghetti." And let me add that goes double for Petits Soufflés with Vanilla Crème de la Crane.

NILES:

Food is also associated with positive emotions, which explains your tendency to overorder when it's my turn to pick up the check.

FRASIER:

You can't type that in.

NILES:

I have the keyboard, I can type what I want. I could type the Magna Carta just waiting for you to get to the point.

FRASIER:

The point is, the human animal has developed numerous coping mechanisms to deal with the stress and strain of daily life: exercise, meditation, split personality . . .

NILES:

Calling in for those mental Band-Aids you dispense on the radio.

FRASIER:

Spending ninety dollars an hour to whine on your couch while you daydream about Daphne.

NILES:

Touché.

FRASIER:

But now, thanks to this gourmet guide to mental health, they can save a bundle, not to mention hours on the couch, by allowing their inner child to wallow in Frasier's Baked Fudge with Kahlúa Cream.

NILES:

Or free their ids to sublimate on Pita Niçoise pour Niles and a steaming cup of Mexican Café au Lait. Like I always say, "If coffee be the food of love, brew on."

FRASIER:

I've never heard you say that.

NILES:

I know, I just thought we should end on a pithy note.

FRASIER:

How about, "Man does not live by Tossed Salads and Scrambled Eggs alone."

NILES:

I said pithy, not abstruse. Perhaps we should just mention that all these recipes can be adapted for a curmudgeonly parent by sprinkling with just a tad of crushed pork rinds?

FRASIER:

Why don't we just say they're so good even Maris eats them.

NILES:

And open ourselves to a lawsuit?

FRASIER:

You're right, we don't want to oversell it. We need something simple yet elegant, like a quote from *Ecclesiastes*. "A man hath no better thing under the sun than to eat, and to drink, and to be merry."

NILES:

I have a better one. "Never eat more than you can lift."

FRASIER:

Voltaire?

NILES:

Miss Piggy.

FRASIER:

That's not going in.

NILES:

Is so.

FRASIER:

Is not.

NILES:

I wonder what one of Dad's Mud Slide Malts would do to your precious suede sofa.

FRASIER:

Try it and you'll be wearing Coffee-Toffee Parfait on that single-breasted Hugo Boss.

NILES:

You wouldn't dare!

FRASIER:

Try me.

FRASIER & NILES:

Food fight!

Man Can Live
By Bread Alone

Daphne Moon-Style Muffins

1½ cups unbleached all-purpose flour

½ cup sugar

¼ cup cornmeal

¼ cup wheat germ

2 tablespoons baking powder

½ teaspoon salt

1½ cups unprocessed bran

½ cup granola cereal

2 cups buttermilk

2½ tablespoons vegetable oil

2 tablespoons peanut butter

2 large eggs, lightly beaten

Combine first 6 ingredients in a large bowl; make a well in center of mixture, and set aside.

Combine bran, granola cereal, and buttermilk; stir well, and let stand 5 minutes. Add oil, peanut butter, and eggs, stirring well. Add to dry ingredients, stirring just until moistened. Spoon into greased muffin pans, filling two-thirds full. Bake at 400° for 25 minutes. Remove from pans immediately. Yield: 1½ dozen.

DAPHNE:
What's the matter? Your aura's just darkened. It's sort of an eggplanty color.

FRASIER:
I'm fine.

DAPHNE:
No you're not. Anything darker than an asparagus spells trouble.

Dried Cherry Muffins

½ cup unsalted butter or margarine, softened

¾ cup sugar

2 large eggs

2 teaspoons grated lemon rind

2 tablespoons lemon juice

2 cups all-purpose flour

1 teaspoon baking soda

½ teaspoon salt

1 cup buttermilk

⅔ cup chopped dried cherries

½ cup chopped walnuts, toasted

Beat butter at medium speed of an electric mixer until creamy; gradually add sugar, beating well. Add eggs, one at a time, beating after each addition. Stir in lemon rind and juice.

Combine flour, soda, and salt; add to butter mixture alternately with buttermilk, beginning and ending with flour mixture. Stir just until blended after each addition. Gently stir in cherries and walnuts.

Spoon batter into lightly greased muffin pans, filling three-fourths full.

Bake at 400° for 20 minutes or until lightly browned. Remove from pans immediately. Yield: 15 muffins.

Key Lime Muffins

2	cups all-purpose flour		2	large eggs, lightly beaten
1	tablespoon baking powder		¼	cup vegetable oil
½	teaspoon salt		1	teaspoon grated lime rind
1	cup sugar		¼	cup Key lime juice
⅓	cup milk			

Combine first 4 ingredients in a large bowl; make a well in center of mixture. Combine milk and remaining ingredients; add to dry ingredients, stirring until moistened. Spoon into greased muffin pans, filling three-fourths full. Bake at 400° for 18 minutes or until browned. Remove from pans immediately. Yield: 1 dozen.

NILES:
   Good morning, Frasier.

FRASIER GRUNTS IN REPLY. A WAITRESS PASSES.

NILES (CONT'D):
   Cara mia, prego uno mezzo latte decaffinato. And a bran muffin. No, due bran muffins. I burned up a lot of energy last night . . . a lot of energy . . . And I have to replenish my body.

FRASIER:
   Niles, is that a love bite on your neck?

NILES:
   Hang the euphemism, Frasier. Call a spade a spade. It's a hickey.

FRASIER:
   Hmm. Well, when one considers Maris's minimal lung capacity, that's quite a feat.

Honey Granola Muffins

1½ cups biscuit and baking mix
1   cup firmly packed brown sugar
1   teaspoon ground cinnamon
1   cup oats and honey granola
     cereal with almonds

½   cup raisins
1   large egg, lightly beaten
¾   cup milk
1   tablespoon vegetable oil
Vegetable cooking spray

Combine first 3 ingredients in a bowl; stir in cereal and raisins. Make a well in center of mixture; set aside.

Combine egg, milk, and oil; add to flour mixture, stirring just until moistened. (Batter will be thin.)

Coat muffin pans with cooking spray; spoon batter into pans, filling three-fourths full.

Bake at 375° for 15 to 20 minutes or until golden. Remove from pans immediately. Yield: 16 muffins.

DAPHNE:

Oh, that was 1983, the happiest summer of my life. Three whole months in Paris. I spent my evenings at the cafés and my afternoons working as a ticket taker at the Eiffel Tower. It was so broadening. To this day I can still say "No spitting off the tower" in twelve different languages.

Basil Biscuits

1	package active dry yeast	¼	teaspoon salt
2	tablespoons warm water (105° to 115°)	2	tablespoons sugar
1	cup buttermilk	½	cup shortening
2½	cups all-purpose flour	¼	cup finely chopped fresh basil
1½	teaspoons baking powder	2	tablespoons finely chopped oil-packed sundried tomatoes
½	teaspoon baking soda		

Combine yeast and warm water in a 2-cup liquid measuring cup; let stand 5 minutes. Stir in buttermilk, and set aside.

Combine flour and next 4 ingredients in a large bowl; cut in shortening with a pastry blender until shortening is the size of peas. Add buttermilk mixture, basil, and tomatoes, stirring with a fork until dry ingredients are moistened. (Dough will resemble cottage cheese and be sticky.) Turn dough out onto a floured surface, and knead lightly 4 or 5 times.

Roll dough to ½-inch thickness; cut with a 2½-inch round cutter. Place biscuits on a lightly greased baking sheet. Cover and let rise in a warm place (85°), free from drafts, 30 minutes.

Bake at 450° for 10 to 12 minutes or until browned. Yield: 1 dozen.

Essence of Rosemary Biscuits

4   cups biscuit and baking mix
1   tablespoon fresh or 1½
    teaspoons dried rosemary,
    crushed

1⅓ cups milk
¼   cup butter or margarine,
    melted

Combine biscuit mix and rosemary in a large bowl. Add milk, stirring with a fork until dry ingredients are moistened. Turn dough out onto a lightly floured surface, and knead lightly 3 or 4 times.

Roll dough to ½-inch thickness; cut with a 2-inch round cutter. Place biscuits on a lightly greased baking sheet. Bake at 450° for 8 minutes or until lightly browned. Brush with melted butter. Yield: 3 dozen.

WAITER:
Are you ready to order?

FRASIER:
I'll have a black coffee.

NILES:
You'll have to forgive my brother. He just came in on the noon stage. Double decaf nonfat latte, medium foam, dusted with the faintest whisper of cinnamon.

THE WAITER LEAVES.

FRASIER:
Well, I hope as long as I live I never become that insufferably pretentious.

NILES:
Too late.

Coconut Biscuits à la Crane

2	cups all-purpose flour	³/₄	cup flaked coconut, toasted
1	tablespoon baking powder	¹/₃	cup shortening
¹/₂	teaspoon salt	1	cup milk
2	tablespoons sugar	¹/₂	teaspoon vanilla extract

Combine first 5 ingredients in a large bowl; cut in shortening with a pastry blender until mixture is crumbly. Combine milk and vanilla; add to dry ingredients, stirring with a fork until dry ingredients are moistened. (Dough will be sticky.)

Drop dough, 2 tablespoons at a time, onto a lightly greased baking sheet. Bake at 450° for 10 minutes or until golden. Yield: about 1 dozen.

FRASIER:
    I need my coffee.

FRASIER POURS HIMSELF SOME COFFEE AND TAKES A SIP. IT STINKS.

FRASIER (CONT'D):
    (WINCING) This isn't my coffee. Where's my finely ground Kenya blend from Starbucks?

MARTIN:
    That's it. Daphne put an eggshell and some allspice in it.

FRASIER:
    And didn't it just dress it up.

HE POURS CUP INTO THE SINK.

MARTIN:
    I like it. It's got zing.

Cranberry Scones with a Skosh of Cloves

2½ cups all-purpose flour

2 teaspoons baking powder

½ teaspoon salt

½ cup sugar

½ teaspoon ground cloves

¼ cup butter or margarine

1 cup whipping cream

¾ cup fresh or frozen cranberries, coarsely chopped

Whipped cream (optional)

Combine first 5 ingredients in a large bowl; cut in butter with a pastry blender until mixture is crumbly.

Reserve 1 tablespoon whipping cream; add remaining whipping cream and cranberries to flour mixture, stirring just until moistened.

Turn dough out onto a lightly floured surface; knead 5 or 6 times. Shape into an 8-inch circle. Cut into 8 wedges, and place on a lightly greased baking sheet. Prick wedges with a fork 3 or 4 times, and brush with reserved 1 tablespoon whipping cream.

Bake at 425° for 18 minutes or until lightly browned. Serve warm with whipped cream, if desired. Yield: 8 scones.

Ham & Cheese Biscuits

Vegetable cooking spray

1½ cups chopped ham (about
    ½ pound)

2 cups all-purpose flour

1 cup (4 ounces) shredded
    extra-sharp Cheddar cheese

2 teaspoons baking powder

Dash of ground red pepper

1 cup milk

Coat a medium-size nonstick skillet with cooking spray; place over medium heat until hot. Add ham; sauté 3 minutes. Combine ham, flour, and next 3 ingredients in a bowl. Add milk, stirring with a fork just until dry ingredients are moistened.

Drop dough by heaping tablespoons onto a baking sheet coated with cooking spray. Bake at 400° for 22 minutes. Yield: 1 dozen.

FRASIER:

Daphne, Dad, there's something we should get clear. I am not a morning person. I need to ease into my day slowly. First, I need my coffee. Sans eggshells or anything else one tends to pick out of the garbage. Then I have a light low-fat, high-fiber breakfast. Finally I sit down and read a crisp, new newspaper. If I'm robbed of the richness of my morning routine, I cannot function, my radio show suffers, and, like ripples in a pond, so do the many listeners who rely on my advice to help them through their troubled lives. I'm sorry if I sound priggish, but I've grown comfortable with that part of myself. It is the magic that is me.

MARTIN: (TO DAPHNE)

Get used to it.

Ham & Cheese Biscuits

Sugared Currant Scones

Sugared Currant Scones

2	cups all-purpose flour		½	cup sour cream
2	teaspoons baking powder		1	large egg, lightly beaten
½	teaspoon baking soda		⅔	cup currants
¼	teaspoon salt		2	teaspoons milk
3	tablespoons sugar		1½	tablespoons sugar
⅓	cup butter or margarine			

Combine first 5 ingredients in a medium bowl; stir well. Cut in butter with a pastry blender until mixture is crumbly. Add sour cream and egg, stirring just until dry ingredients are moistened. Stir in currants.

Turn dough out onto a lightly floured surface, and knead lightly 4 or 5 times. Pat dough into a 7-inch circle on a greased baking sheet. Brush top with milk; sprinkle with 1½ tablespoons sugar. Cut circle into 6 wedges, using a sharp knife.

Bake at 400° for 14 to 16 minutes or until lightly browned. Serve scones warm with jam or honey butter. Yield: 6 scones.

FRASIER:
(WITHOUT LOOKING AT EDDIE) You're not getting any of my scone, so just forget it. And it's really good, too. Look, you may think you can wear me down, but as far as I'm concerned, you're not even here. (EDDIE KEEPS STARING) Oh, for God's sake, here. Get fat.

Cappuccino Biscotti

2 cups all-purpose flour
½ teaspoon baking powder
½ teaspoon baking soda
½ teaspoon salt
1 cup sugar
⅓ cup chopped walnuts
¼ cup cocoa
½ teaspoon ground cinnamon

2 teaspoons instant coffee granules
2 teaspoons hot water
1 teaspoon vanilla extract
2 large eggs, lightly beaten
1 egg white, lightly beaten
Vegetable cooking spray

Combine first 8 ingredients in a large bowl. Combine coffee granules and hot water in a small bowl. Stir in vanilla and next 2 ingredients; add to flour mixture, stirring until blended.

Turn dough out onto a lightly floured surface, and knead lightly 7 or 8 times. Shape dough into a 16-inch-long roll. Place roll on a baking sheet coated with cooking spray, and flatten roll to 1-inch thickness.

Bake at 325° for 30 minutes. Remove roll from baking sheet to a wire rack, and let cool 10 minutes. Cut roll diagonally into 30 (½-inch) slices, and place, cut sides down, on baking sheet. Bake at 325° for 10 minutes. Turn slices over, and bake 10 additional minutes (biscotti will be slightly soft in center but will harden as they cool). Remove from baking sheet; let cool completely on wire rack. Yield: 2½ dozen.

Savory Biscotti with a Smidgen of Smoked Cheddar

2   cups all-purpose flour
2   tablespoons yellow cornmeal
1   teaspoon baking powder
1   teaspoon salt
1   teaspoon sugar
½   teaspoon dried basil

½   cup sour cream
2   tablespoons butter, melted
3   egg whites
½   cup (2 ounces) shredded
    smoked Cheddar cheese
Vegetable cooking spray

Combine first 6 ingredients in a large bowl. Combine sour cream and next 2 ingredients in a small bowl; stir with a wire whisk until blended. Stir in cheese; add to flour mixture, stirring until blended (dough will be crumbly).

Turn dough out onto a lightly floured surface, and knead lightly 7 or 8 times. Shape dough into a 16-inch-long roll. Place roll on a baking sheet coated with cooking spray, and flatten roll to 1-inch thickness.

Bake at 350° for 30 minutes. Remove roll from baking sheet to a wire rack, and let cool 10 minutes. Cut roll diagonally into 24 (½-inch) slices, and place, cut sides down, on baking sheet. Reduce oven temperature to 325°, and bake 15 minutes. Turn slices over, and bake 15 additional minutes (biscotti will be slightly soft in center but will harden as they cool). Remove from baking sheet; let cool completely on wire rack. Yield: 2 dozen.

Hazelnut Tea Bread

⅓	cup hazelnuts	1	egg white, lightly beaten
1	cup coarsely shredded peeled pear (about 2 medium)	1½	cups all-purpose flour
¾	cup sugar	½	cup whole-wheat flour
3	tablespoons vegetable oil	1¼	teaspoons baking powder
½	teaspoon grated lemon rind	½	teaspoon baking soda
½	teaspoon vanilla extract	½	teaspoon salt
1	large egg, lightly beaten	¾	teaspoon ground cinnamon

Place hazelnuts on a baking sheet. Bake at 350° for 15 minutes, stirring once. Turn nuts out onto a towel. Roll up towel, and rub off skins. Chop nuts; set aside.

Combine pear and next 6 ingredients in a large bowl; stir well. Combine hazelnuts, all-purpose flour, and next 5 ingredients; add to pear mixture, stirring just until moistened.

Spoon batter into a lightly greased 8½- x 4½- x 3-inch loafpan. Bake at 350° for 1 hour and 5 minutes or until a wooden pick inserted in center comes out clean. Let cool in pan 10 minutes on a wire rack; remove from pan, and let cool completely on wire rack. Yield: 1 loaf.

Macadamia Banana Bread

2¼ cups all-purpose flour

1 tablespoon plus ½ teaspoon baking powder

½ teaspoon salt

1 cup firmly packed brown sugar

1½ teaspoons ground cinnamon

1¼ cups mashed ripe banana

⅓ cup milk

3 tablespoons vegetable oil

1 large egg

1 teaspoon white vinegar

1 cup macadamia nuts, coarsely chopped and toasted

Combine first 5 ingredients in a large bowl; make a well in center of mixture. Combine banana, milk, oil, egg, and vinegar; beat with a wire whisk until blended. Add to dry ingredients, stirring just until moistened. Stir in macadamia nuts.

Spoon batter into a greased 9- x 5- x 3-inch loafpan. Bake at 350° for 1 hour or until a wooden pick inserted in center comes out clean. Let cool in pan 10 minutes on a wire rack; remove from pan, and let cool completely on wire rack. Yield: 1 loaf.

Mocha Nervosa Walnut Bread

2	cups all-purpose flour		2	large eggs, lightly beaten
½	teaspoon baking soda		⅓	cup butter or margarine, melted
¼	teaspoon salt			
1	cup sugar		1	cup (6 ounces) semisweet chocolate morsels
½	cup cocoa			
¼	cup instant coffee granules		½	cup chopped walnuts, toasted
1¼	cups sour cream			

Combine first 6 ingredients in a medium bowl; stir well. Combine sour cream, eggs, and butter in a large bowl; stir well. Add flour mixture to sour cream mixture, stirring until blended. Stir in chocolate morsels and walnuts. Pour batter into a greased and floured 9- x 5- x 3-inch loafpan.

Bake at 350° for 50 to 55 minutes or until a wooden pick inserted in center comes out clean. Let cool in pan 10 minutes on a wire rack; remove from pan, and let cool completely on wire rack. Yield: 1 loaf.

Bodacious Buttermilk Pancakes

2	cups all-purpose flour		2	tablespoons sugar
2½	teaspoons baking powder		2	large eggs, lightly beaten
1	teaspoon baking soda		2	cups buttermilk
¾	teaspoon salt		¼	cup vegetable oil

Combine first 5 ingredients; stir well. Combine eggs, buttermilk, and oil; add to flour mixture, stirring just until dry ingredients are moistened.

For each pancake, pour ¼ cup batter onto a hot, lightly greased griddle. Cook pancakes until tops are covered with bubbles and edges look cooked; turn and cook other side. (Any unused batter may be refrigerated in a tightly covered container up to 1 week. If refrigerated batter is too thick, add milk or water to reach desired consistency.) Serve pancakes warm with fruit-flavored syrup. Yield: 19 (4-inch) pancakes.

FRASIER:
What would you like, cappuccino, latte?

MARTIN:
(TO WAITRESS) Coffee. Black. And don't put anything fancy in it.

WAITRESS:
We have two special coffees today . . .
(MARTIN GLARES AT HER)

WAITRESS (CONT'D):
I'll surprise you.

Deep-Dish Cheesecake Coffee Cake

3	cups biscuit and baking mix	2	large eggs
¼	cup sugar	½	cup sugar
½	cup milk	½	teaspoon vanilla extract
¼	cup butter or margarine, melted	¼	cup strawberry preserves
1	(8-ounce) package cream cheese, softened		

Combine biscuit mix, ¼ cup sugar, milk, and butter; stir vigorously 30 seconds. Turn dough out onto a lightly floured surface; knead 4 or 5 times. Pat dough evenly in bottom and up sides of an ungreased 9-inch round cakepan; set aside.

Combine cream cheese, eggs, ½ cup sugar, and vanilla; beat at medium speed of an electric mixer until smooth. Pour over dough; bake at 350° for 30 to 35 minutes. Remove from oven; let stand 10 minutes. Spread preserves over top. Serve warm. Yield: one 9-inch coffee cake.

MARTIN:
No, no. And I can pay for my own coffee. How much is it?

FRASIER:
A dollar fifty.

MARTIN:
For coffee? What kind of world are we living in?

Silken Sour Cream Coffee Cake

½ cup butter or margarine, softened

½ cup shortening

1¼ cups sugar

2 large eggs

1 (8-ounce) carton sour cream

2 cups all-purpose flour

1 teaspoon baking powder

½ teaspoon baking soda

½ teaspoon salt

1 teaspoon vanilla extract

½ cup chopped pecans

2 tablespoons sugar

1 teaspoon instant coffee granules

Sifted powdered sugar

Beat butter and shortening at medium speed of an electric mixer 2 minutes or until creamy. Gradually add 1¼ cups sugar, beating at medium speed 5 to 7 minutes. Add eggs, one at a time, beating just until yellow disappears. Add sour cream, mixing until blended.

Combine flour and next 3 ingredients; gradually add to butter mixture, mixing until blended. Stir in vanilla. Spoon half of batter into a greased and floured 8-inch tube pan.

Combine chopped pecans, 2 tablespoons sugar, and coffee granules; sprinkle half of mixture over batter. Repeat procedure with remaining batter and pecan mixture.

Bake at 350° for 55 minutes. Cool in pan on a wire rack 10 to 15 minutes; remove from pan, and let cool completely on wire rack. Sprinkle with powdered sugar. Yield: one 8-inch coffee cake.

Maple Cream-Coconut Pastries

1   cup firmly packed brown sugar
⅓   cup maple syrup
¼   cup butter or margarine,
        melted
½   cup chopped pecans
1   (8-ounce) package cream
        cheese, softened

¼   cup sifted powdered sugar
2   tablespoons butter or
        margarine, softened
½   cup flaked coconut
2   (10-ounce) cans refrigerated
        flaky biscuits

Combine first 4 ingredients in a bowl, stirring well. Spread mixture into an ungreased 13- x 9- x 2-inch pan.

Combine cream cheese, powdered sugar, and 2 tablespoons butter in a small mixing bowl. Beat at medium speed of an electric mixer until blended. Stir in coconut.

Separate biscuit dough into 20 pieces. Roll each biscuit on a lightly floured surface to a 4-inch circle. Spread 1 tablespoon cream cheese mixture evenly onto each biscuit, and roll up jellyroll fashion. Place in prepared pan, seam side down, in two long rows.

Bake at 350° on lowest rack in oven for 25 minutes or until biscuits are brown. Let cool in pan 3 minutes. Turn pastries out onto a serving platter. Top with any remaining maple glaze mixture. Yield: 20 pastries.

LET'S DO LUNCH

Quiche for the Fine-Boned

Pastry for 9-inch pie
1½ cups (6 ounces) shredded
    Monterey Jack cheese
1 cup (4 ounces) shredded mild
    Cheddar cheese, divided
1 (4-ounce) can chopped green
    chiles, undrained
⅓ cup finely chopped onion
⅓ cup drained, chopped canned
    mushrooms
3 large eggs
1 cup half-and-half
¼ teaspoon salt
⅛ teaspoon ground cumin
Dash of Worcestershire sauce
½ cup finely chopped tomatoes

Roll pastry to ⅛-inch thickness on a floured surface. Place pastry in a 9-inch deep-dish pieplate. Fold edges under; crimp. Prick bottom and sides with a fork. Bake at 400° for 10 minutes or until browned. Let cool on a wire rack.

Sprinkle Monterey Jack cheese and ½ cup Cheddar cheese over bottom of pastry shell. Sprinkle chiles, onion, and mushrooms over cheese. Combine eggs and next 4 ingredients; beat with a wire whisk until blended. Pour egg mixture into pastry shell. Sprinkle with remaining ½ cup Cheddar cheese. Bake, uncovered, at 350° for 45 minutes or until set and browned. Let stand 15 minutes before serving. Top each serving with tomato. Yield: one 9-inch quiche.

Pita Niçoise pour Niles

½ pound new potatoes

¼ pound haricots verts (French baby green beans)

⅔ cup mayonnaise

2 large cloves garlic, crushed

1 teaspoon dried oregano

1 teaspoon lemon juice

½ teaspoon salt

½ teaspoon sugar

3 (6⅛-ounce) cans solid white tuna, drained well and chunked

1 small purple onion, finely chopped

½ cup Niçoise olives or other small black olives, sliced

2 tablespoons red wine vinegar

½ teaspoon freshly ground pepper

3 large pita bread rounds

Red leaf lettuce

3 Roma tomatoes, thinly sliced

2 tablespoons capers

Cook potatoes in a small amount of boiling water 10 to 15 minutes or until tender. Drain; let cool to touch, and coarsely chop potatoes. Trim stem ends of beans. Arrange beans in a vegetable steamer over boiling water. Cover and steam 3 to 4 minutes or until crisp-tender. Plunge in ice water to stop cooking process; drain and cut beans into ¾-inch pieces.

Combine mayonnaise and next 5 ingredients, stirring well. Combine potatoes, beans, tuna, onion, and olives in a large bowl. Sprinkle with vinegar and pepper; toss gently. Stir in mayonnaise mixture. Cut pita rounds in half crosswise; line each half with lettuce and tomato. Spoon tuna mixture evenly into pita halves. Sprinkle with capers. Yield: 6 servings.

Chicken Salad au Vin

6 cups chopped cooked chicken
1¼ cups sliced celery
1 (8-ounce) can pineapple tidbits, drained
1¼ cups mayonnaise or salad dressing
2½ tablespoons dry white wine
¾ teaspoon salt
¾ teaspoon curry powder

2 Gala apples, thinly sliced
1 cantaloupe, thinly sliced
½ pound green grapes
1 pint strawberries
1 cup blackberries
Curly leaf lettuce leaves
¾ cup coarsely chopped walnuts, toasted
Garnish: celery leaves

Combine first 3 ingredients in a large bowl; set aside.

Combine mayonnaise and next 3 ingredients. Add to chicken mixture, tossing to coat. Cover and chill 1 to 2 hours.

Arrange apple and next 4 ingredients on a lettuce-lined platter; top with chicken mixture. Sprinkle with walnuts. Garnish, if desired. Yield: 6 servings.

Crab Louis

1	cup mayonnaise or salad dressing	1	head curly leaf lettuce, shredded
¼	cup chili sauce	2	pounds fresh crabmeat, drained and flaked
¼	cup chopped green onions	2	large tomatoes, cut into wedges
1	teaspoon lemon juice	4	hard-cooked eggs, cut into wedges
¼	teaspoon salt		
¼	cup whipping cream, whipped		

Combine first 5 ingredients in a large bowl. Fold in whipped cream; set dressing aside. Place shredded lettuce in a serving bowl or on a platter; arrange crabmeat, tomato wedges, and eggs on lettuce. Spoon 2 tablespoons dressing over salad; serve with remaining dressing. Yield: 8 to 10 servings.

FRASIER:

Aren't you going to join me?

NILES:

I would, but I don't like to break my routine. I come in every day at five-fifteen, order one double decaf nonfat latte and read my paper. First the news, then the financial section, and finally a fleeting glance at the obituaries. Maris so loves those estate sales. This leaves me fifteen minutes to contemplate the events of the day, pay my check and get back to my office in time for my obsessive compulsives group, those poor tortured souls.

Grilled Vegetable Salad
With a Splash of Balsamic Vinegar

⅓	cup white balsamic vinegar	½	pound carrots, scraped
2	tablespoons olive oil	1	large sweet red pepper, seeded
2	shallots, finely chopped	1	large sweet yellow pepper, seeded
1	teaspoon dried Italian seasoning	2	zucchini
¼	teaspoon salt	2	large yellow squash
¼	teaspoon pepper	1	large onion
1½	teaspoons molasses		

Combine first 7 ingredients in a large bowl. Set aside.

Cut carrots and remaining vegetables into large pieces.

Add vegetables to vinegar mixture, tossing to coat. Let stand 30 minutes, stirring occasionally. Drain vegetables, reserving vinegar mixture. Arrange vegetables in a grill basket.

Cook, covered with grill lid, over medium-hot coals (350° to 400°) 15 to 20 minutes, turning occasionally.

Return vegetables to reserved vinegar mixture, tossing gently. Cover and refrigerate at least 8 hours. Yield: 6 cups.

Grilled Vegetable Salad with a Splash of Balsamic Vinegar

Sweet Onion-Smothered Hamburger

Sweet Onion-Smothered Hamburgers

2   cups thinly sliced onion,
      separated into rings
Vegetable cooking spray
¼   cup chili sauce
2   tablespoons grape jelly
1   pound ground round
¼   cup dry breadcrumbs
¼   cup chili sauce

1   tablespoon instant minced
      onion
¼   teaspoon ground pepper
1   clove garlic, minced
4   hamburger buns, split
4   curly leaf lettuce leaves
1   large tomato, sliced

Place sliced onion in a large nonstick skillet coated with cooking spray. Cover and cook over medium heat 10 minutes or until onion is limp and golden, stirring occasionally. Reduce heat to low, and add ¼ cup chili sauce and grape jelly. Cover and cook 5 minutes.

Combine beef and next 5 ingredients in a bowl; stir well. Divide mixture into 4 equal portions, shaping each into a ½-inch-thick patty. Prepare grill or broiler. Place patties on grill rack or broiler pan coated with cooking spray, and cook 4 minutes on each side or until done.

Line the bottom halves of buns with a lettuce leaf and tomato slices; top each with a patty, ¼ cup onion mixture, and top half of bun. Yield: 4 servings.

Grilled Shiitakes on Rosemary Focaccia

1	package active dry yeast	Vegetable cooking spray	
1¼	cups warm water (105° to 115°)	2	tablespoons olive oil
3½	cups all-purpose flour, divided	4	cloves garlic, minced
1	teaspoon coarse salt, divided	Grilled Shiitakes	
¼	cup butter, melted		
½	cup chopped fresh rosemary, divided		

Combine yeast and warm water in a 2-cup liquid measuring cup; let stand 5 minutes. Combine yeast mixture, 2 cups flour, and ½ teaspoon salt in a large bowl, stirring well.

Cover and let rise in a warm place (85°), free from drafts, 1 hour or until doubled in bulk. Punch dough down, and stir in remaining flour, butter, and ¼ cup chopped rosemary.

Turn dough out onto a lightly floured surface, and knead 10 minutes.

Divide dough into thirds; roll each portion into a 9-inch circle on baking sheets coated with cooking spray.

Brush dough evenly with olive oil; sprinkle evenly with remaining ¼ cup rosemary, ½ teaspoon salt, and garlic. Prick dough generously with a fork.

Bake at 400° for 18 to 20 minutes. Top each focaccia with Grilled Shiitakes before serving. Yield: 3 servings.

Note: Coarse salt enhances the flavors in this bread. Substitute regular salt, if desired.

Grilled Shiitakes

1	pound large fresh shiitake mushrooms	¼	cup chopped fresh parsley
½	cup butter or margarine, melted	½	teaspoon freshly ground pepper
4	cloves garlic, minced	¼	teaspoon salt

Remove stems from mushrooms; discard stems. Combine butter and next 4 ingredients; spread evenly on both sides of mushroom caps. Cook, without grill lid, over medium-hot coals (350° to 400°) 8 minutes, turning once. Slice or chop shiitakes, if desired. Yield: 2½ cups.

DAPHNE:
> *If you need to save a bit you should do what I do and cut out coupons. We've got tons.*

NILES SITS WITH DAPHNE AND PERUSES THE COUPONS.

NILES:
> *Coupons—what a wonderful way to economize. I'll just clip the gourmet ones and give them to my personal shopper.*

Prosciutto-and-Fontina Panini

1   (5.25-ounce) package focaccia
    or 1 (8-ounce) package Boboli
8   very thin slices prosciutto
    (about 2 ounces)
¼   cup (1 ounce) shredded fontina
    cheese

1   cup trimmed arugula
2   (⅛-inch-thick) red onion
    slices, separated into rings
2   teaspoons balsamic vinegar
⅛   teaspoon pepper

Slice each bread round in half horizontally. Divide prosciutto between bottom halves of bread, and top each bread half with cheese, arugula, and onion slices. Drizzle vinegar over sandwiches, and sprinkle with pepper; cover with top halves of bread. Wrap sandwiches tightly in foil, and bake at 300° for 15 minutes. Yield: 2 servings.

FRASIER:
Dad, what are you doing?

MARTIN:
I'm teaching Eddie a new trick.

FRASIER:
With my twenty-six dollar a pound imported prosciutto?

MARTIN:
Believe me, it's worth it.

FRASIER:
Not unless he can sing the love duet from "Tosca."

Crispy Potato, Tomato, and Mozzarella Squares

1   (10-ounce) can refrigerated pizza crust dough
Vegetable cooking spray
1   tablespoon fresh rosemary
½   teaspoon crushed red pepper
2   large cloves garlic, minced
¾   pound round red potatoes, cut into ¼-inch-thick slices
2   tablespoons balsamic vinegar
¼   teaspoon salt
3   Roma tomatoes, sliced
18 basil leaves
6   ounces part-skim mozzarella cheese, thinly sliced

Unroll dough, and press into bottom of a greased 13- x 9- x 2-inch baking dish. Spray dough with cooking spray; sprinkle with rosemary, red pepper, and garlic. Bake at 400° for 15 minutes or until browned. Let cool in pan on a wire rack.

Place potato slices in a medium saucepan; add water to cover. Bring to a boil; boil 5 minutes or until potatoes are crisp-tender. Drain; pat dry with paper towels. Place potato slices in a shallow dish. Combine vinegar and salt; pour over potato slices, tossing to coat. Arrange potato slices in a single layer on a greased baking sheet. Bake at 450° for 18 to 20 minutes or until browned, turning after 10 minutes.

Cut crust into 12 squares. Arrange potato slices over 6 squares. Top potato with tomato slices, basil, and cheese. Top with remaining crust squares, garlic side down. Wrap sandwiches in heavy-duty plastic wrap. Place a pan holding 2 or 3 (1-pound) cans on top of sandwiches to flatten, and refrigerate up to 4 hours. Yield: 6 servings.

Chichi Grilled Cheese

1   cup (4 ounces) shredded sharp
      Cheddar cheese
1   cup finely chopped Gala apple
½   cup minced pimiento-stuffed
      olives

¼   cup mayonnaise
8   slices honey wheat bread
Melted butter or margarine

Combine first 4 ingredients in a bowl; stir well. Spread mixture evenly on 1 side of 4 slices of bread to within ¼ inch of edges. Top with remaining slices of bread; brush top slices with melted butter, and invert onto a hot griddle. Immediately brush other sides of sandwiches with melted butter; cook over medium heat until golden. Turn sandwiches, and brown other sides. Yield: 4 servings.

Grilled Spinach Fondue Sandwiches

1   (10-ounce) package frozen
       chopped spinach, partially
       thawed
½   cup dry sherry
1½ cups (6 ounces) shredded Swiss
       cheese
1   teaspoon ground nutmeg,
       divided

2   tablespoons mayonnaise
¼   teaspoon salt
¼   teaspoon pepper
12 (1-inch-thick) slices French
       bread
2   tablespoons butter or
       margarine, softened

Combine spinach and sherry in a small saucepan, and cook 4½ minutes; drain.

Combine spinach mixture, cheese, ½ teaspoon nutmeg, and next 3 ingredients. Spoon evenly onto half of bread slices; top with remaining bread slices.

Spread half of butter on outside of 1 side of each sandwich; sprinkle with half of remaining nutmeg. Invert sandwiches onto a hot nonstick skillet or griddle. Cook sandwiches over medium heat until golden.

Spread remaining butter on ungrilled side, and sprinkle with remaining nutmeg. Turn sandwiches and brown other sides. Yield: 6 servings.

Smoked Turkey-Roasted Pepper Sandwiches

2 tablespoons softened cream
   cheese
1 tablespoon mayonnaise
1 tablespoon spicy brown
   mustard
⅛ teaspoon pepper
¼ cup chopped commercial
   roasted red peppers, drained

2 tablespoons sliced green onions
8 slices pumpernickel bread
¾ pound sliced smoked turkey
   breast
¼ cup alfalfa sprouts

Combine first 4 ingredients; stir in red peppers and green onions.

Spread mixture evenly on one side of bread slices. Layer turkey and alfalfa sprouts on 4 slices of bread; top with remaining bread slices. Cut in half. Serve immediately. Yield: 4 servings.

Italian Chicken-Mozzarella Melt

4	skinned and boned chicken breast halves	4	French rolls, halved and toasted
2	tablespoons olive oil	1	small zucchini, shredded
1/4	teaspoon salt	1/2	cup (2 ounces) shredded mozzarella cheese
1/2	teaspoon dried oregano, divided	1/4	cup grated Parmesan cheese
1	cup pizza sauce		
1 1/2	teaspoons fresh or 1/2 teaspoon dried basil		

Brush each piece of chicken with olive oil; sprinkle with salt and 1/4 teaspoon oregano.

Cook chicken in a greased nonstick skillet over medium-high heat about 4 minutes on each side or until done. Set chicken aside.

Combine pizza sauce, basil, and remaining 1/4 teaspoon oregano in skillet; cook over medium-high heat until thoroughly heated. Remove from heat; add chicken, and keep warm.

Place rolls on a baking sheet; spread sauce evenly on bottom half of each roll; top evenly with chicken, zucchini, and cheeses.

Broil 3 inches from heat (with electric oven door partially opened) 2 to 3 minutes or until cheese melts. Cover with tops of rolls. Yield: 4 servings.

Bulldog's Big BLT Croissants

1	(3-ounce) package cream cheese, softened	1	tablespoon chopped fresh or 1 teaspoon dried basil
1	(3-ounce) package goat cheese, softened	4	large croissants, cut in half horizontally
¼	cup chopped oil-packed sun-dried tomatoes	8	slices bacon, cooked
		1	cup torn red leaf lettuce

Combine cream cheese and goat cheese, stirring until smooth; stir in tomatoes and basil. Spread cheese mixture evenly on each croissant half, and place on an ungreased baking sheet. Bake at 325° for 5 minutes or until cheese mixture begins to melt. Remove from oven, and place 2 strips of bacon on bottom half of each croissant. Top with lettuce and tops of croissants. Serve immediately. Yield: 4 servings.

FRASIER:
Oh come on, Roz, don't you think there's just the tiniest possibility that the reason Bulldog asked you to be his producer was because he . . . you know, maybe he wanted to . . .

ROZ:
Wanted to what?

NILES:
Dip his biscotti in your latte. (TO DAPHNE) I'm sorry you had to hear that.

Martin's Mile-High Ham-and-Cheese Hoagie

1   (1-pound) round loaf
      sourdough bread or
      6 hoagie rolls
½   cup mayonnaise
2½ teaspoons dried Italian
      seasoning
½   teaspoon pepper
1   large onion, thinly sliced
2   green or sweet red peppers, cut
      into thin strips

1   stalk celery, sliced
1   tablespoon olive oil
1   pound cooked ham, thinly
      sliced (about 25 slices)
1½ cups (6 ounces) shredded
      Cheddar and mozzarella
      cheese blend

Slice off top third of bread loaf; set top aside. Hollow out bottom section, leaving a ½-inch shell. Combine mayonnaise, Italian seasoning, and pepper. Brush inside of bread shell with half of mixture. Set shell and remaining mixture aside.

Cook onion, pepper strips, and celery in olive oil in a large skillet over medium-high heat until tender, stirring often.

Arrange half of ham in bread shell, and top with half of vegetable mixture; sprinkle with half of cheese. Spread remaining mayonnaise mixture over cheese. Repeat layers with remaining vegetable mixture, ham, and cheese. Replace bread top. Wrap sandwich in heavy-duty aluminum foil.

Bake at 400° for 30 minutes or until thoroughly heated. Cut sandwich into wedges, and serve immediately. Yield: 6 servings.

Cajun Salmon on Sourdough

¼ cup plus 2 tablespoons butter
    or margarine, melted

1 teaspoon coarse sea salt

1 teaspoon dried basil

1 teaspoon dried thyme

1 teaspoon paprika

1 teaspoon black pepper

½ teaspoon ground red pepper

4 (6-ounce) salmon steaks, 1 inch
    thick

8 slices sourdough bread, toasted
    or grilled

Combine first 7 ingredients in a small bowl; stir well. Brush butter mixture evenly over both sides of salmon steaks. Grill, covered, over hot coals (400° to 500°) 7 minutes on each side or until fish flakes easily when tested with a fork. Serve on toasted sourdough bread. Yield: 4 servings.

FRASIER:

(TO NILES) You, ice fishing? You get a runny nose watching figure skating on TV.

NILES:

Say what you will, Frasier, but I like to think of myself as a man of the great al fresco.

JUST BRING
TWO FORKS

Chocolate-Hazelnut Biscotti

2	large eggs	¼	teaspoon salt
⅔	cup sugar	1½	tablespoons cocoa
1	tablespoon Frangelico	⅔	cup hazelnuts, chopped and toasted
2	cups sifted cake flour		
1½	teaspoons baking powder		Vegetable cooking spray

Beat eggs at medium speed of an electric mixer until foamy. Gradually add sugar, beating at high speed until mixture is thick and pale. Add liqueur, beating until blended. Combine flour and next 3 ingredients; fold into egg mixture. Fold in nuts. Cover and chill 30 minutes.

Coat a cookie sheet with cooking spray. Divide dough into 3 portions; spoon portions onto cookie sheet 2 inches apart. Shape each portion of dough into an 8-inch long roll. Cover and chill 30 minutes; reshape dough, if necessary.

Bake at 375° for 20 minutes. Remove rolls to wire racks to cool. Cut rolls diagonally into ½-inch-thick slices. Lay slices flat on an ungreased cookie sheet. Bake at 375° for 5 minutes; turn slices over, and bake 5 additional minutes. Remove to wire racks to cool. Yield: 3½ dozen.

Strawberries 'n' Roz Romanoff

1	cup whipping cream	2	tablespoons lemon juice
1	pint vanilla ice cream, softened	2	quarts strawberries, hulled and
¼ to ½ cup Curaçao or other			halved
	orange-flavored liqueur	¼	cup sifted powdered sugar

Beat whipping cream in a small mixing bowl at high speed of an electric mixer until soft peaks form; set aside.

Beat ice cream in a large mixing bowl until smooth. Gently fold in whipped cream. Stir in liqueur and lemon juice; chill.

Combine strawberries and powdered sugar; toss gently. Divide evenly into wine goblets. Top with whipped cream mixture. Yield: 12 servings.

ROZ:
Hey, Frasier.

FRASIER:
Hi, Roz. May I?

HE SITS AT HER TABLE AS THE WAITRESS APPROACHES WITH ROZ'S ORDER.

WAITRESS:
Here we are, one double tall latte and a slice of pecan pie with extra whipped cream. Anything else?

FRASIER:
Perhaps a blood pressure cuff? (THEN) A nonfat cappuccino, please.

Chocolate Bags in a Raspberry Pool

1   (10-ounce) package frozen
    raspberries in light syrup,
    thawed and undrained
1¼ cups sifted powdered sugar,
    divided
1   (17¼-ounce) package frozen
    puff pastry sheets, thawed

1   cup semisweet chocolate
    morsels
1   cup vanilla milk morsels or
    white chocolate, chopped
1   cup chopped pecans

Combine raspberries and 1 cup powdered sugar in a container of an electric blender; process until smooth, stopping once to scrape down sides. Pour raspberry mixture through a wire-mesh strainer into a bowl; discard seeds. Cover and chill.

Roll each pastry sheet into a 12-inch square on a lightly floured surface; cut each sheet of pastry into 4 squares.

Combine chocolate morsels, vanilla morsels, and pecans; place evenly in middle of each pastry square. (Reserve some morsel mixture for garnish, if desired.) Pull up sides of pastry to enclose morsel mixture; twist ends just above morsels, pinching to seal at "neck" and spreading open top edges of pastry. Place filled bags on an ungreased baking sheet. Bake at 425° for 20 minutes, covering loosely with aluminum foil after 10 minutes to prevent excess browning.

Spoon raspberry sauce evenly onto 8 dessert plates; set aside. Sprinkle baked pastries with remaining ¼ cup powdered sugar, and place a pastry bag in center of each plate on sauce. Sprinkle any reserved morsel mixture on plates. Serve immediately. Yield: 8 servings.

Chocolate Bag in a Raspberry Pool

Pears en Croûte

Pears en Croûte

2   (15-ounce) packages
        refrigerated piecrusts
5 or 6 firm ripe pears, unpeeled
1   egg yolk

1   tablespoon water
Caramel Sauce
Garnish: fresh mint leaves

Unfold piecrusts, one at a time; place on a floured surface, and roll each into a 10-inch square. Cut each square into 1-inch strips. Starting at bottom of 1 pear, begin wrapping with 1 pastry strip, overlapping strip ¼ inch as you cover pear. Continue wrapping by moistening ends of strips with water and joining to previous strip until pear is covered. Repeat procedure with remaining pears and pastry strips. Place pears on a greased baking sheet. Combine egg yolk and 1 tablespoon water; brush on pastry. Bake at 350° for 1 hour or until tender. Spoon Caramel Sauce onto each plate; top with a pear. Garnish, if desired. Yield: 5 or 6 servings.

Caramel Sauce

1   (12-ounce) jar caramel ice
        cream topping
1   (14-ounce) can sweetened
        condensed milk

2   tablespoons lemon juice
¼   cup Cointreau or other
        orange-flavored liqueur

Combine caramel topping and milk in top of a double boiler; bring water to a boil. Reduce heat to low; cook, stirring constantly, until smooth. Stir in lemon juice and Cointreau. Yield: 2½ cups.

Caramel-Brownie Cheesecake

1¾ cups vanilla wafer crumbs
⅓ cup butter, melted
1 (14-ounce) package caramels
1 (5-ounce) can evaporated milk
2½ cups coarsely crumbled unfrosted brownies
3 (8-ounce) packages cream cheese, softened

1 cup firmly packed brown sugar
3 large eggs
1 (8-ounce) carton sour cream
2 teaspoons vanilla extract
Garnishes: whipped cream, chocolate-lined wafer rolls, chocolate coffee beans

Combine vanilla wafer crumbs and butter; firmly press into bottom and 2 inches up sides of a lightly greased 9-inch springform pan. Bake at 350° for 5 minutes. Let cool on a wire rack.

Combine caramels and milk in a small heavy saucepan; cook over low heat, stirring often, until caramels melt. Pour caramel mixture over crust. Sprinkle crumbled brownies over caramel.

Beat cream cheese at medium speed of an electric mixer 2 minutes or until fluffy. Gradually add brown sugar, mixing well. Add eggs, one at a time, beating after each addition just until blended. Stir in sour cream and vanilla. Pour batter over brownies. Bake at 350° for 50 minutes to 1 hour or until almost set. Remove from oven; let cool on a wire rack. Cover and chill at least 4 hours. Remove sides of pan. Garnish, if desired. Yield: one 9-inch cheesecake.

Note: Buy prepackaged unfrosted brownies from a bakery, or prepare your favorite mix; let cool, and crumble enough to yield 2½ cups.

Cream Cheese Pound Cake

1½ cups butter, softened

1 (8-ounce) package cream
cheese, softened

3 cups sugar

6 large eggs

1½ teaspoons vanilla extract

3 cups all-purpose flour

⅛ teaspoon salt

Beat butter and cream cheese at medium speed of an electric mixer 2 minutes or until mixture is creamy. Gradually add sugar, beating 5 to 7 minutes. Add eggs, one at a time, beating just until yellow disappears. Add vanilla, mixing well.

Combine flour and salt; gradually add to butter mixture, beating at low speed just until blended after each addition. Pour batter into a greased and floured 10-inch tube pan. Fill a 2-cup, ovenproof measuring cup with water; place in oven with tube pan.

Bake at 300° for 1 hour and 45 minutes or until a wooden pick inserted in center of cake comes out clean. Let cool in pan on a wire rack 10 to 15 minutes; remove from pan, and cool completely on wire rack. Yield: one 10-inch cake.

Irish Cream-and-Coffee Pound Cake

1½ cups butter or margarine, softened

3 cups sugar

6 large eggs

1½ tablespoons instant coffee granules

¼ cup boiling water

½ cup Irish cream liqueur

4 cups all-purpose flour

1 teaspoon vanilla extract

1 teaspoon almond extract

Irish Cream Glaze

3 tablespoons sliced almonds, toasted

Beat butter at medium speed of an electric mixer about 2 minutes or until soft and creamy. Gradually add sugar, beating at medium speed 5 to 7 minutes. Add eggs, one at time, beating just until yellow disappears.

Dissolve coffee granules in boiling water; stir in liqueur. Add flour to butter mixture alternately with coffee mixture, beginning and ending with flour mixture. Mix at low speed just until blended after each addition. Stir in flavorings.

Pour batter into a greased and floured 13-cup Bundt pan. Bake at 300° for 1 hour and 40 minutes or until a wooden pick inserted in center of cake comes out clean. Let cool in pan on a wire rack 10 to 15 minutes; remove from pan, and cool 30 minutes on wire rack. Brush with Irish Cream Glaze, and sprinkle with toasted almonds. Let cool completely. Yield: one 10-inch cake.

Irish Cream Glaze

1	teaspoon instant coffee granules	1½	tablespoons Irish cream liqueur
2	tablespoons boiling water	⅔	cup sifted powdered sugar

Dissolve coffee granules in boiling water; add liqueur and powdered sugar, stirring until blended. Yield: about ½ cup.

FRASIER:
What are your coffees of the day?

WAITRESS:
Zimbabwe and Kenya.

FRASIER:
I'll have a Zimbabwe latte.

NILES:
And I'll have a Kenya cappuccino.

FRASIER:
Something tells me that's the closest we're ever going to come to a safari.

Chocolate Chiffon Cake with Coffee Buttercream

6   (1-ounce) squares bittersweet
     chocolate, chopped
¾   cup water
1   cup butter, softened
2   cups sugar
4   large eggs
2   teaspoons vanilla extract

2½   cups sifted cake flour
2   teaspoons baking soda
⅛   teaspoon salt
1½   cups sour cream
     Coffee Buttercream
     Chocolate-covered coffee beans

Combine chocolate and water in a heavy saucepan; cook over low heat, stirring constantly, until chocolate melts.

Beat butter at medium speed of an electric mixer until creamy; gradually add sugar, beating well. Add eggs, one at a time, beating after each addition. Add chocolate mixture and vanilla; beat 1 minute or just until combined.

Combine flour, soda, and salt; add to chocolate mixture alternately with sour cream, beginning and ending with flour mixture. Mix at low speed just until blended after each addition. Pour batter into 3 greased and floured 9-inch round cakepans.

Bake at 350° for 25 to 30 minutes or until a wooden pick inserted in center comes out clean. Let cool in pans on wire racks 10 minutes; remove from pans, and cool completely on wire racks.

Spread Coffee Buttercream between layers and on top and sides of cake. Arrange coffee beans on top of cake. Yield: one 3-layer cake.

Coffee Buttercream

3 tablespoons boiling water	1 cup butter, softened
4 to 5 tablespoons instant coffee granules	6 cups sifted powdered sugar

Combine water and coffee granules, stirring until coffee dissolves. Let cool.

Beat butter at medium speed of an electric mixer until creamy; gradually add sugar and coffee mixture, beating until blended. Yield: 2½ cups.

NILES:
I'll have a grande half-caf latte with a whisper of cinnamon on top and for my father a plain coffee. I cannot emphasize the word "plain" enough. No foam. No cinnamon. No exotic flavors. If it's not plain I take no responsibility for the consequences.

WAITRESS:
How about a biscotti?

NILES:
All right, but when you bring it, call it a cookie.

WAITRESS:
(TO NILES) Here's your latte. (TO MARTIN) And here's your coffee and your . . . (LOOKS AT NILES) cookie.

MARTIN:
Oh great, you got me a biscotti.

NILES:
This day is full of surprises.

Frasier's Baked Fudge with Kahlúa Cream

2 cups sugar
¾ cup cocoa
½ cup all-purpose flour
5 large eggs
1 cup plus 2 tablespoons butter
    or margarine, melted

2½ teaspoons vanilla extract
1⅓ cups chopped pecans, toasted
Kahlúa Cream

Combine first 3 ingredients in a large mixing bowl, stirring well. Add eggs; beat at medium speed of an electric mixer until smooth. Add butter and vanilla, beating well. Stir in pecans. Spoon mixture into 8 lightly greased 6-ounce custard cups. Place in a 13- x 9- x 2-inch pan; add hot water to pan to depth of 1 inch. Bake, uncovered, at 300° for 1 hour. Remove custard cups from water. Let stand 10 minutes. Serve warm with Kahlúa Cream. Yield: 8 servings.

Kahlúa Cream

1 cup whipping cream
½ cup sifted powdered sugar

3 tablespoons Kahlúa

Beat cream in a large mixing bowl until foamy; gradually add powdered sugar, beating until soft peaks form. Fold in Kahlúa. Cover and chill. Yield: 2⅓ cups.

Martin's Ice Cream & Candy Bar Concoction

2	cups cream-filled chocolate sandwich cookie crumbs (about 20 cookies, crushed)	1½	quarts vanilla ice cream, slightly softened
½	cup unsalted, dry-roasted peanuts, coarsely chopped	1	(11.75-ounce) jar hot fudge sauce, divided
¼	cup butter or margarine, melted	1	(12-ounce) jar hot caramel sauce, divided
6	(2.07-ounce) chocolate-coated caramel-peanut nougat bars		

Combine first 3 ingredients; press into bottom and up sides of a lightly greased 9-inch deep-dish pieplate. Bake at 350° for 10 minutes; set aside to cool completely.

Chop candy bars into small pieces, and reserve 2 tablespoons. Fold remaining candy into ice cream, and spread evenly into crust.

Drizzle with 2 tablespoons fudge sauce and 2 tablespoons caramel sauce; sprinkle with reserved candy. Cover and freeze until firm.

Remove pie from freezer 20 minutes before serving. Serve pie with remaining fudge and caramel sauce. Yield: 8 servings.

Chocolate Dessert in Crème Anglaise

16 (1-ounce) squares semisweet
    chocolate, chopped
⅔ cup butter or margarine
5 large eggs
2 tablespoons sugar

2 tablespoons all-purpose flour
Crème Anglaise
Garnishes: chocolate curls, fresh
    mint sprigs

Line the bottom of a 9-inch springform pan with parchment paper; set aside.

Melt chopped chocolate and butter in a large heavy saucepan over medium-low heat, stirring often. Remove from heat, and let cool slightly. Gradually add chocolate mixture to eggs, beating at medium speed of an electric mixer 10 minutes. Fold in sugar and flour. Pour mixture into prepared pan.

Bake at 400° for 15 minutes. (Cake will not be set in center.) Remove from oven. Let cool; cover and chill thoroughly.

Spoon Crème Anglaise onto each dessert plate; place a wedge of Chocolate Dessert on each plate. Garnish, if desired. Yield: 10 servings.

Crème Anglaise

2	cups milk	5	egg yolks
½	cup sugar, divided	½	teaspoon vanilla extract

Combine milk and ¼ cup sugar in a heavy nonaluminum saucepan. Bring to a simmer over medium heat. Beat remaining ¼ cup sugar and egg yolks at high speed of an electric mixer until pale and mixture forms a ribbon.

Gradually add hot milk mixture to egg mixture, whisking until blended; return to saucepan. Cook over medium-low heat, stirring constantly, until custard thickens and coats a spoon. Remove from heat; strain. Stir in vanilla. Cover and chill. Yield: 2 cups.

ROZ:

I'd like to meet the idiot who came up with these. Take a grape, let it shrivel into a disgusting little wart and cover it with perfectly good chocolate. Ah, what the hell, I'll just suck off the chocolate.

FRASIER:

Be sure to save what's left and maybe you can make some wine.

Chocolate Truffle Mousse with Raspberry Sauce

8   (1-ounce) squares semisweet
    chocolate
¼   cup light corn syrup
¼   cup butter or margarine
2   egg yolks, lightly beaten

1   cup whipping cream, divided
2   tablespoons powdered sugar
½   teaspoon vanilla extract
Raspberry Sauce
Garnish: chocolate curls

Combine first 3 ingredients in a heavy saucepan; cook over low heat, stirring constantly, until chocolate melts.

Combine egg yolks and ¼ cup whipping cream. Gradually stir about ½ cup chocolate mixture into yolk mixture; add to remaining chocolate mixture, stirring constantly. Cook over medium-low heat 1 minute or until a thermometer registers 160°. Remove from heat; let cool to room temperature.

Beat remaining ¾ cup whipping cream until foamy; gradually add powdered sugar, beating until soft peaks form. Stir in vanilla.

Stir ½ cup whipped cream mixture into chocolate mixture; fold in remaining whipped cream mixture. Spoon into 4 stemmed glasses; cover and chill at least 8 hours. Serve with Raspberry Sauce. Garnish glasses, if desired. Yield: 4 servings.

Raspberry Sauce

1	(10-ounce) package frozen raspberries, thawed	2	teaspoons cornstarch
		⅓	cup light corn syrup

Place raspberries in container of an electric blender; process 1 minute or until smooth, stopping once to scrape down sides. Pour mixture through a wire-mesh strainer into a small saucepan, discarding seeds. Add cornstarch, stirring well; stir in corn syrup.

Cook over medium heat, stirring constantly, until mixture boils. Boil 1 minute, stirring constantly. Remove from heat; let cool. Yield: 1⅓ cups.

FRASIER:
Niles, I think you'll find this Courvoisier is the perfect brandy to top off our evening.

NILES:
It was an exquisite meal, marred only by the lack of even one outstanding Cognac on their carte de digestifs.

FRASIER:
But think about it, Niles. What's the one thing better than an exquisite meal? An exquisite meal with one tiny flaw we can pick at all night.

NILES:
Quite right. Let's savor it.

Sabayon

15 egg yolks
½ cup sugar
3 tablespoons Marsala wine
2 cups fresh or frozen
   raspberries, thawed
2 cups fresh or frozen
   blueberries, thawed

2 cups fresh or frozen
   blackberries, thawed
Sweetened whipped cream
Garnish: fresh mint sprigs

Bring water to a boil in bottom of a double boiler. Place egg yolks in top of double boiler on countertop; beat at high speed of a hand-held electric mixer until foamy. Gradually add sugar, 1 tablespoon at a time, beating until thick and pale. Gradually add Marsala, beating mixture well. Place over boiling water, and cook, stirring constantly with a wire whisk, 10 minutes or until mixture reaches 160°. Remove top of double boiler from heat, and place in a large bowl of ice water, stirring with whisk until mixture is cold.

Arrange fruit in compotes or individual serving dishes; immediately spoon sauce over fruit. Dollop with whipped cream, and garnish, if desired. Serve immediately. Yield: 10 servings.

Note: Although the name is French, this cooked custard is a classic Italian dessert. (The Italians refer to it as "zabaglione.")

Caramel-Coffee Flan

¾ cup sugar
2 large eggs
2 egg yolks
1 (14-ounce) can sweetened
   condensed milk

1 cup half-and-half
1 teaspoon instant coffee
   granules

Place sugar in a small heavy saucepan. Cook over medium heat, stirring constantly with a wooden spoon, until sugar crystallizes into lumps (about 15 minutes). Continue cooking, stirring constantly, until sugar melts and turns a light golden brown (about 15 minutes). Quickly pour hot caramel mixture into an ungreased 8-inch round cakepan, tilting to coat bottom evenly. Set aside (mixture will harden).

Combine eggs and remaining ingredients in a large bowl; beat with a wire whisk until coffee granules dissolve. Pour egg mixture over caramelized sugar in cakepan.

Place cakepan in a large shallow baking dish. Pour hot water into baking dish to depth of 1 inch. Cover with aluminum foil, and bake at 350° for 55 minutes or until a knife inserted near center of flan comes out clean. Remove pan from water, and let cool. Cover and chill at least 8 hours.

To serve, loosen edge of custard with a spatula, and invert onto a serving plate. Yield: 6 servings.

White Chocolate-Macadamia Nut Crème Brûlée

4   ounces white chocolate, chopped

2   cups whipping cream, divided

5   egg yolks

½   cup sugar

1   teaspoon vanilla extract

¼   cup plus 1 tablespoon chopped macadamia nuts, toasted

½   cup firmly packed brown sugar

Garnish: white chocolate shavings

Combine white chocolate and ½ cup whipping cream in a heavy saucepan; cook over low heat, stirring constantly, until chocolate melts. Add remaining 1½ cups whipping cream, egg yolks, ½ cup sugar, and vanilla, stirring with a wire whisk until sugar dissolves and mixture is smooth. Place 1 tablespoon chopped macadamia nuts in each of 5 (5- x 1-inch) round individual baking dishes. Pour custard evenly over nuts. Place dishes in a large roasting pan. Add hot water to pan to depth of ½ inch.

Bake at 275° for 1 hour and 10 minutes or until almost set. Cool custards in water in pan on a wire rack. Remove from pan; cover and chill custards at least 8 hours.

Sprinkle about 1½ tablespoons brown sugar evenly over each custard; place custards in pan.

Broil 5½ inches from heat (with electric oven door partially opened) until brown sugar melts. Let stand 5 minutes to allow brown sugar to harden. Garnish, if desired. Yield: 5 servings.

White Chocolate-Macadamia Nut Crème Brûlée

Tiramisù

Tiramisù

6	egg yolks	2	teaspoons instant coffee granules
1¼	cups sugar		
1¼	cups mascarpone cheese (see note)	1½	tablespoons brandy
		2	(3-ounce) packages ladyfingers
1¾	cups whipping cream		Garnishes: whipped cream, grated unsweetened chocolate
¾	cup water		

Combine egg yolks and sugar in top of a double boiler; beat at medium speed of an electric mixer until thick and lemon colored. Bring water to a boil; reduce heat to low, and cook 8 to 10 minutes or until mixture reaches 160°, stirring constantly. Remove from heat. Add mascarpone, and beat until smooth.

Beat whipping cream in a medium bowl until soft peaks form; fold into cheese mixture.

Combine water, coffee granules, and brandy; brush on cut side of ladyfingers. Line sides and bottom of a trifle bowl or 3-quart soufflé dish with 36 ladyfingers; pour in half of filling. Layer remaining ladyfingers on top; cover with remaining filling. Garnish, if desired; cover and chill 8 hours. Yield: 10 to 12 servings.

Note: As a substitute for mascarpone cheese, combine 2 (8-ounce) packages cream cheese, ⅓ cup sour cream, and ¼ cup whipping cream; beat well. Use 1¼ cups mixture for recipe, reserving remainder for other uses.

Petits Soufflés with Vanilla Crème de la Crane

Butter

Sugar

3   tablespoons butter or
        margarine

3   tablespoons all-purpose flour

¾   cup half-and-half

¼   cup sugar

4   large eggs, separated

2   tablespoons vanilla extract

2   tablespoons sugar

Sifted powdered sugar

Vanilla Crème de la Crane

Coat the bottom and sides of 8 (4-ounce) baking dishes with butter; sprinkle with sugar. Set aside.

Melt 3 tablespoons butter in a large saucepan over medium heat; add flour, stirring until smooth. Cook 1 minute, stirring constantly. Add half-and-half, stirring constantly. Stir in ¼ cup sugar. Cook over medium heat, stirring constantly, until thickened. Remove from heat, and set hot mixture aside.

Beat egg yolks until thick and pale. Gradually stir about one-fourth of hot mixture into yolks; add to remaining hot mixture, stirring constantly. Cook 2 minutes; stir in vanilla. Let cool 15 to 20 minutes.

Beat egg whites in a large bowl at high speed of an electric mixer until foamy. Gradually add 2 tablespoons sugar, 1 tablespoon at a time, beating until soft peaks form. Gently fold about one-fourth of egg whites into half-and-half mixture; fold in remaining whites. Spoon into prepared dishes.

Bake at 350° for 20 minutes or until puffed and set. Sprinkle with powdered sugar. Serve immediately with Vanilla Crème de la Crane. Yield: 8 servings.

Vanilla Crème de la Crane

½	vanilla bean	2	cups whipping cream
1	cup sugar	7	egg yolks
2	teaspoons cornstarch		

Position knife blade in food processor bowl; add vanilla bean and sugar; process until bean is finely chopped.

Combine sugar mixture and cornstarch in a heavy saucepan; gradually add whipping cream. Cook over low heat until sugar dissolves. Set hot mixture aside.

Beat egg yolks until thick and pale; gradually stir about one-fourth of hot mixture into yolks. Add to remaining mixture, stirring constantly.

Cook over medium heat, stirring constantly, until thickened. Pour through a wire-mesh strainer into a 1-quart bowl, discarding solids. Cover and refrigerate up to 3 days. Serve leftover sauce over fresh fruit, pound cake, or ice cream. Yield: 3 cups.

NILES:
> *(TO WAITRESS) Nonfat, half-caf latte, with a sprinkle of cinnamon and chocolate. I'm feeling madcap today.*

WAITRESS:
> *Maybe instead of nonfat milk you should go for the two percent?*

NILES:
> *I said madcap, not hell-bent.*

Mexican Mocha Ice Cream

1	cup half-and-half	4	egg yolks
3	(1-ounce) squares semisweet chocolate, coarsely chopped	⅔	cup sugar
		1	tablespoon butter or margarine
2	teaspoons instant coffee granules	1	cup whipping cream, whipped
		2	tablespoons Kahlúa

Combine half-and-half, chocolate, and coffee granules in a small saucepan; cook over low heat until chocolate melts, stirring occasionally. Set aside.

Beat egg yolks and sugar at high speed of an electric mixer until thick and pale. Gradually stir in chocolate mixture; cook over low heat, stirring constantly, 10 minutes or until thickened. Remove from heat; stir in butter. Let cool 15 minutes; stir in whipped cream and liqueur.

Pour mixture into freezer container of a 2-quart electric ice cream freezer. Freeze according to manufacturer's instructions.

Pack freezer with additional ice and rock salt, and let ripen 1 hour before serving. Yield: 1 quart.

Lemon Gelato

1 cup sugar	⅔ cup fresh lemon juice
1 tablespoon grated lemon rind	1½ cups plain yogurt
⅛ teaspoon salt	Fresh mint sprigs (optional)

Combine first 4 ingredients in a bowl; stir until sugar dissolves. Add yogurt; stir well. Pour mixture into freezer container of an ice cream freezer. Freeze according to manufacturer's instructions. Garnish with mint, if desired. Yield: about 3 cups.

Serving suggestion: Trim bottoms of 5 whole lemons so they stand up. Cut off top third of the lemons, and scoop out the pulp, leaving the shells intact. Place lemon shells, upside down, on paper towels until well drained. Spoon frozen gelato into lemon shells, and freeze until firm.

Orange Sorbet

2½ cups water

1   cup sugar

Rind strips from 2 oranges

2⅔ cups fresh orange juice

⅓   cup fresh lemon juice

Grated orange rind (optional)

Combine water and sugar in a saucepan, and bring to a boil. Add orange rind strips; reduce heat, and simmer 5 minutes. Discard orange rind strips; remove liquid from heat, and let cool completely.

Add orange juice and lemon juice; stir well. Pour mixture into freezer container of a 2-quart electric ice cream freezer. Freeze according to manufacturer's instructions. Allow sorbet to ripen 1 hour. Garnish, if desired. Yield: 1½ quarts.

Fresh Peach Sorbet

4   **cups chopped peeled peaches**
     (about 2½ pounds)

¾   **cup sugar**

½   **cup Sauternes or other sweet**
     white wine

Place peaches and sugar in a food processor. Add wine, and process until smooth. Pour mixture into freezer container of a 2-quart electric ice cream freezer. Freeze according to manufacturer's instructions. Allow sorbet to ripen 1 hour. Yield: 5 cups.

Brandied Pumpkin Ice Cream Pie
With Malted Pecans

1½	cups graham cracker crumbs	⅛	teaspoon ground ginger
½	teaspoon ground cinnamon	2	tablespoons brandy
2	egg whites, lightly beaten	4	cups vanilla ice cream, softened
1	tablespoon water		
1	cup canned mashed pumpkin	3	tablespoons chopped pecans, toasted
⅓	cup firmly packed brown sugar		
1	teaspoon ground cinnamon	2	tablespoons malted milk powder
¼	teaspoon ground allspice		
¼	teaspoon ground nutmeg		

Combine the first 4 ingredients in a bowl; toss with a fork until moistened. Press into bottom and up sides of a greased 9-inch pieplate. Bake at 350° for 10 minutes. Let cool on a wire rack.

Combine pumpkin and next 5 ingredients in a bowl; stir well. Stir in brandy. Fold in ice cream to create a marbled effect. Spoon pumpkin mixture into prepared crust. Cover loosely, and freeze 8 hours.

Place pie in refrigerator 20 minutes before serving to soften. Place pecans and malted milk powder in a food processor, and process until pecans are ground. Sprinkle pecan mixture around edge of pie. Yield: one 9-inch pie.

Coffee-Toffee Parfaits

3   cups Coffee Ice Milk
Toffee Crunch

6   tablespoons frozen whipped
    topping, thawed

Spoon ¼ cup Coffee Ice Milk into each of 6 parfait glasses; top each with 2 tablespoons Toffee Crunch. Repeat layers; top each parfait with 1 tablespoon whipped topping. Freeze until ready to serve. Yield: 6 servings.

Coffee Ice Milk

2   cups boiling water
4   teaspoons instant coffee
    granules
¾   cup sugar

⅛   teaspoon salt
1   (4-ounce) carton egg substitute
1   cup evaporated skimmed milk
½   cup 2% low-fat milk

Combine boiling water and coffee granules; stir well. Cover and chill.

Combine sugar, salt, and egg substitute in a bowl; beat at medium speed of an electric mixer 3 minutes or until sugar is dissolved. Add coffee; beat 2 minutes. Add milks; beat well.

Pour mixture into freezer container of a 2-quart ice cream freezer. Freeze according to manufacturer's instructions. Transfer to another freezer-safe container; cover and freeze at least 1 hour. Yield: 7 cups.

Toffee Crunch

½ cup firmly packed dark brown sugar

¼ cup sliced almonds

2 teaspoons butter or margarine, softened

Vegetable cooking spray

Combine sugar, almonds, and butter in food processor; pulse 10 times or until nuts are finely chopped. Press mixture into a 7-inch circle on a baking sheet coated with cooking spray. Broil 1 minute until bubbly but not burned. Remove from oven, and let stand 5 minutes. Gently turn toffee over, using a wide spatula, and broil an additional minute. (Watch closely as toffee broils—let it bubble, but not burn.) Remove from oven, and let cool. Break toffee mixture into ½-inch pieces. Yield: 1½ cups.

(See photograph of parfait on page 91)

Chocolate-Pecan Tart with a Soupçon of Cinnamon

2 cups pecan pieces
¼ cup firmly packed brown sugar
¼ teaspoon ground cinnamon
2 tablespoons butter or margarine, softened

1 (12-ounce) package semisweet chocolate morsels
½ cup half-and-half
Caramel Sauce (page 57)

Position knife blade in food processor bowl; add pecans, and pulse 5 or 6 times or until finely chopped. Add brown sugar, cinnamon, and butter; process 30 seconds, stopping once to scrape down sides. Press mixture evenly into bottom and about ½ inch up sides of a 9-inch tart pan.

Bake at 325° for 25 minutes; set aside.

Combine chocolate morsels and half-and-half in a saucepan; cook over medium heat, stirring constantly, until chocolate melts and mixture is smooth. Pour into tart shell.

Cover and chill at least 2 hours. Serve with warm Caramel Sauce. Yield: one 9-inch tart.

Daphne's Midnight Delights

⅔ cup boiling water

2 teaspoons instant coffee granules

1¾ cups all-purpose flour

⅓ cup cocoa

¼ cup sugar

Dash of salt

¾ cup butter, cut into pieces

2 cups (12 ounces) semisweet chocolate morsels, melted

⅔ cup sugar

2 tablespoons butter, melted

2 tablespoons milk

2 teaspoons Kahlúa or strongly brewed coffee

2 large eggs, lightly beaten

½ cup chopped pecans or walnuts

½ cup whipping cream

1 tablespoon powdered sugar

Combine ⅔ cup boiling water and coffee granules, stirring well; let cool. Reserve 2 teaspoons. Combine flour and next 3 ingredients; cut in butter with a pastry blender until crumbly. Sprinkle remaining coffee mixture, 1 tablespoon at a time, evenly over flour mixture; stir with a fork until dry ingredients are moistened.

Turn dough out onto a floured surface; knead 3 times. Wrap in wax paper; chill 1 hour. Shape into ¾-inch balls; press into greased miniature (1¾-inch) muffin pans, using a tart tamper. Cover and chill. Combine melted chocolate and next 4 ingredients, stirring until smooth; stir in eggs and pecans. Spoon 1 teaspoonful of mixture into each tart shell. Bake at 350° for 20 minutes. Cool on wire racks 15 minutes; remove from pans, and cool completely on racks. Combine reserved 2 teaspoons coffee mixture, cream, and powdered sugar; beat at medium speed of an electric mixer until soft peaks form. Dollop onto each tart just before serving. Yield: 4 dozen.

White Chocolate Chess Tart

½   (15-ounce) package
    refrigerated piecrusts
1   (4-ounce) white chocolate bar,
    chopped
½   cup buttermilk
3   large eggs, lightly beaten

1   tablespoon vanilla extract
1¼ cups sugar
Pinch of salt
3   tablespoons all-purpose flour
1   tablespoon cornmeal

Fit 1 piecrust into a 9-inch tart pan with removable bottom according to package directions; trim edges. Line pastry with aluminum foil, and fill with pie weights or dried beans.

Bake at 450° for 8 minutes. Remove weights and foil; bake 3 to 4 additional minutes. Cool piecrust on a wire rack.

Combine chocolate and buttermilk in a small saucepan; cook over low heat, stirring constantly, until chocolate melts and mixture is smooth. Let cool 15 minutes.

Combine eggs and vanilla in a bowl; gradually stir in chocolate mixture.

Combine sugar and next 3 ingredients; gradually add to chocolate mixture, stirring until blended. Pour mixture into piecrust.

Bake at 325° for 50 minutes or until a knife inserted in center comes out clean. Let cool on a wire rack. Yield: one 9-inch tart.

SOME LIKE IT HOT

Raspberry Milk Shakes

1   (10-ounce) package frozen   ½   cup milk
      raspberries   1   quart vanilla ice cream

Combine frozen raspberries and milk in container of an electric blender; cover and process until smooth. Add ice cream; cover and process until mixture is smooth. Serve immediately. Yield: 5 (1-cup) servings.

Almond-Coffee Freeze

¼   cup amaretto   1½ cups vanilla ice cream
¼   cup Kahlúa   5 to 7 ice cubes

Combine all ingredients in container of an electric blender; cover and process until frothy. Serve immediately. Yield: about 3 (¾-cup) servings.

Icy Rum Coffee Cream

⅓ cup water

¼ cup firmly packed brown
   sugar

2 tablespoons instant coffee
   granules

1½ cups vanilla ice cream

1 cup milk

½ cup dark rum

2 tablespoons Cointreau or other
   orange-flavored liqueur

4 ice cubes

Garnishes: whipped cream,
   chocolate curls

Combine water, brown sugar, and coffee granules in a small saucepan; cook
over low heat, stirring constantly, until sugar and coffee granules dissolve. Let cool
completely. Combine coffee mixture, ice cream, and next 4 ingredients in container of an electric blender; cover and process 30 seconds or until smooth.
Garnish with whipped cream and chocolate curls, if desired. Serve immediately.
Yield: 3 (1-cup) servings.

FRASIER (TO DAPHNE):
> Listen, I know how bleak things can look when you're going
> through a dry spell, but they always end sooner or later.
> I remember once in Boston feeling exactly the way you
> do now—and the very next week I met a lovely, if
> somewhat loquacious, barmaid, fell madly in love and
> got engaged . . . (REALIZING, SADLY) Of course, she
> left me standing at the altar—but the point is I didn't give up. I
> took my poor, battered heart and offered it to Lilith, (THINKS)
> who put it in her little Cuisinart and hit the puree button.

Martin's Mud Slide Malts

1 cup milk
1 teaspoon finely ground
  espresso beans
6 cups vanilla ice cream, divided
½ cup hot fudge topping, divided
½ cup chocolate-flavored instant
  malted milk, divided

¼ cup Kahlúa or strongly brewed
  coffee, cooled
6 cream-filled chocolate
  sandwich cookies, coarsely
  chopped and divided

Combine milk and espresso, stirring well. Pour half of milk mixture into container of an electric blender; add half each of ice cream, fudge topping, malted milk, and liqueur. Cover and process until smooth, stopping once to scrape down sides. Stir in half of chopped cookies. Spoon malts into glasses.

Place remaining half of milk mixture, ice cream, fudge topping, malted milk, and liqueur in container of electric blender. Cover and process until smooth. Stir in remaining chopped cookies. Spoon into glasses. Serve immediately. Yield: 6 (1-cup) servings.

Coffee-Toffee Parfait, (see page 82)

Toffee Coffee

Toffee Coffee

3 cups hot brewed Swiss chocolate-almond coffee

2⅔ tablespoons butterscotch topping

2⅔ tablespoons chocolate syrup

½ teaspoon almond extract

Garnishes: sweetened whipped cream, chopped English toffee-flavored candy bars

For each serving, combine ¾ cup coffee, 2 teaspoons butterscotch topping, 2 teaspoons chocolate syrup, and ⅛ teaspoon almond extract. Stir well. Garnish with whipped cream and chopped candy bar, if desired. Yield: 4 (¾-cup) servings.

FRASIER:
You bought . . . five plaid shirts?

MARTIN:
Hey, we only go around once. See, the way I figure it, with five shirts and five pairs of pants I actually have twenty-five different outfits. (DEMONSTRATES) Throw in a change of belts and we're up to fifty.

FRASIER:
Dear God, the decisions you'll wrestle with each morning.

MARTIN:
I may never have to buy another pair of pants in my lifetime.

NILES:
And what a load off your mind that must be.

Vanilla Coffee Chiller

8 cups hot brewed hazelnut-
  flavored coffee

½ cup sugar

1 tablespoon vanilla extract

2 cups milk

⅔ cup vanilla frozen yogurt,
  softened

Combine coffee, sugar, and vanilla, stirring until sugar dissolves. Stir in milk; cover and chill. For each serving, pour 1 cup coffee mixture into a glass, and top with 1 tablespoon frozen yogurt. Yield: 10 (1-cup) servings.

FRASIER AND NILES ARE STANDING AT THE COUNTER, ORDERING.

COUNTER PERSON:
  What can I get you?

NILES:
  I'll have a decaf, nonfat latte.

FRASIER:
  Make that two.

COUNTER PERSON:
  Got it. (YELLING TO ESPRESSO OPERATOR) Two gutless wonders!

NILES AND FRASIER SHRINK IN EMBARRASSMENT TOWARD THEIR TABLE.

FRASIER:
  Whatever happened to simpler times when they just called it a good ol' cup a Joe?

Crane's Coffee Bracer

1 cup strong, cold brewed coffee	2 tablespoons brandy (optional)
1²⁄₃ cups milk	1 tablespoon chocolate syrup
2 tablespoons instant coffee granules	1 cup club soda, chilled

Pour coffee into 1 ice cube tray; freeze until firm.

Combine milk and coffee granules; stir until granules dissolve. Add brandy, if desired, chocolate syrup, and club soda; stir well. Place coffee ice cubes in individual glasses. Pour coffee over cubes, and serve immediately. Yield: 3 (1-cup) servings.

Iced Hazelnut Café au Lait

6 cups strongly brewed coffee	3 cups milk
7 cups strongly brewed hazelnut-flavored coffee, chilled	¼ cup plus 1 tablespoon sugar

Pour 6 cups brewed coffee into ice cube trays; freeze until firm.

Combine hazelnut-flavored coffee, milk, and sugar; stir until sugar dissolves. Place coffee ice cubes in individual glasses. Pour coffee over cubes, and serve immediately. Yield: 10 (1-cup) servings.

German Chocolate Café au Lait

3½ tablespoons ground Dutch
 Almond coffee

1 cup water

½ cup hot milk

2 tablespoons CocoRibe or other
 coconut-flavored liqueur

2 tablespoons Frangelico or
 other hazelnut-flavored
 liqueur

¼ cup whipped cream

2 teaspoons grated sweet baking
 chocolate

Prepare coffee according to manufacturer's instructions, using 3½ tablespoons ground coffee and 1 cup water. Combine hot milk and liqueurs. Pour hot milk mixture and hot coffee simultaneously into mugs; top with whipped cream and grated chocolate. Yield: 2 (¾-cup) servings.

NILES:
 *Double cappuccino, half-caf, nonfat milk,
 with enough foam to be aesthetically
 pleasing, but not so much that
 it would leave a mustache.*

WAITER:
 Cinnamon or chocolate on that?

NILES: (TO FRASIER)
 They always make this so complicated.

Mexican Café au Lait

1¼ cups milk

¼ cup Kahlúa

1½ cups hot vanilla-flavored coffee

¼ teaspoon ground cinnamon

Combine milk and liqueur in a saucepan; cook over low heat until very warm. Pour hot milk mixture and hot coffee simultaneously into 4 coffee cups. Sprinkle each with cinnamon, and serve immediately. Yield: 3 (1-cup) servings.

NILES:
> Here we are. One triple espresso and one mocha latte.
> (SHOWING FRASIER HIS MOCHA; ANNOYED)
> Do those chocolate shavings look any different to you?

FRASIER:
> No.

NILES:
> Well, they do to me. I think they've switched to
> an inferior domestic brand.

NILES TAKES A SIP AND SCRUNCHES UP HIS NOSE.

NILES (CONT'D):
> Waxy.

HE TAKES HIS HANDKERCHIEF AND DABS HIS LIPS.
FRASIER TAKES THE HANDKERCHIEF FROM HIM.

FRASIER:
> I'll have this sent to the lab for analysis.

Bourbon Java

2	cups hot brewed coffee	2	tablespoons bourbon
2	tablespoons brown sugar		Sugar
2	cups chocolate milk		

Combine coffee and brown sugar, stirring until brown sugar dissolves. Stir in chocolate milk and bourbon; cover and chill.

To serve, dip rims of 4 stemmed glasses in water and then in sugar to coat rims. Pour 1 cup coffee mixture into each glass. Yield: 4 (1-cup) servings.

Café Pontalba

12	cups hot coffee with chicory		Whipped cream
½	cup Kahlúa or crème de cacao		Grated chocolate
12	sugar cubes	12	(4-inch) sticks cinnamon

Combine coffee and liqueur; ladle into cups. Add a sugar cube to each cup. Top each serving with a dollop of whipped cream; sprinkle with chocolate. Serve with cinnamon-stick stirrers. Yield: 12 (1-cup) servings.

Amaretto Espresso

¼ cup semisweet chocolate
    morsels
1½ tablespoons sugar
1 tablespoon water

2 cups hot brewed espresso
¼ cup amaretto
Whipped cream
⅓ cup crushed amaretti cookies

Combine first 3 ingredients in a small saucepan; cook over low heat, stirring constantly, until smooth. Stir in espresso. Remove from heat; stir in amaretto. Pour into espresso or coffee cups; top with whipped cream, and sprinkle with cookies. Yield: 5 (½-cup) servings.

WAITRESS:
Espresso Man says you can choose cinnamon or chocolate or get lost.

NILES:
Perhaps the Espresso Man should be reminded that I have been coming to this establishment almost daily for over four years.

WAITRESS:
Why do you think he said it?

NILES:
Oh, in that case, chef's choice.

Anise-Scented Coffee

½ cup ground coffee

½ teaspoon anise seeds, crushed

2 teaspoons ground cinnamon

½ teaspoon ground cloves

5 cups water

Combine coffee, anise seeds, cinnamon, and cloves in a medium bowl. Place coffee mixture in basket of an electric percolator or a drip coffee maker. Add water to percolator, and brew according to manufacturer's instructions. To serve, pour into individual mugs. Serve hot. Yield: 5 (1-cup) servings.

Cardamom Coffee

2 quarts freshly brewed hot coffee

12 cardamom seeds, crushed

1 medium-size orange, thinly sliced and seeded

Combine all ingredients in a large saucepan; bring to a boil. Cover; reduce heat, and simmer 5 minutes. Strain and serve hot. Yield 8 (1-cup) servings.

Chocolate Malted Coffee

4   cups brewed chocolate
      almond-flavored coffee,
      divided

1¾ cups milk, divided

¼   cup malted milk powder,
      divided

2   tablespoons chocolate syrup,
      divided

Combine half each of all ingredients in container of an electric blender; cover and process until frothy. Repeat procedure with remaining half of ingredients. Serve hot or cold. Yield: 6 (1-cup) servings.

Chocolate-Pecan Coffee

½   cup medium-grind pecan-
      flavored coffee

1   tablespoon cocoa

½   teaspoon ground cinnamon

5   cups water

3   tablespoons chocolate syrup

Combine first 3 ingredients in basket of an electric percolator or drip coffee maker. Add 5 cups water to percolator. Prepare coffee according to manufacturer's instructions. Stir in chocolate syrup. Yield: 5 (1-cup) servings.

Harvest Coffee

¼	cup ground coffee	1	cup milk
1½	teaspoons apple pie spice	2	tablespoons maple syrup
3½	cups water		Garnish: 4 (3-inch) sticks cinnamon

Combine coffee and apple pie spice in basket of an electric percolator or drip coffee maker. Add 3½ cups water to percolator. Prepare coffee according to manufacturer's instructions.

Combine milk and syrup in a small saucepan; cook over medium heat until thoroughly heated (do not boil). Pour ¾ cup coffee and ¼ cup milk mixture into each mug; stir well. Garnish each serving with a cinnamon stick, if desired. Yield: 4 (1-cup) servings.

FRASIER:
I'll have a nonfat decaf latte, please. What am I saying? I'll have a full-fat mocha, extra whipped cream and you can throw on some bacon if you like.

Coffee-Eggnog Punch

2	(1-quart) cartons refrigerated eggnog	¼	cup Kahlúa or other coffee-flavored liqueur
¼	cup firmly packed brown sugar	1	cup whipping cream
2	tablespoons instant coffee granules	¼	cup sifted powdered sugar
¼	teaspoon ground cinnamon	1	teaspoon vanilla extract
1	cup brandy		Ground cinnamon

Combine first 4 ingredients in a large bowl; beat at low speed of an electric mixer until coffee granules dissolve. Stir in brandy and Kahlúa; cover and chill 1 to 2 hours. Pour into a punch bowl.

Combine whipping cream, powdered sugar, and vanilla; beat at high speed until stiff peaks form. Dollop whipped cream onto punch; sprinkle lightly with additional cinnamon. Yield: 9 (1-cup) servings.

FRASIER (TO ROZ):
Have you ever been to Orsini's?

ROZ:
Are you kidding? My typical date's idea of a gourmet evening is take-out, make out and home by Letterman.

Roz's Velvet Punch

6	cups brewed coffee	¾	cup chocolate syrup
3	cups half-and-half	1	pint coffee ice cream
1	cup Cookies 'n' Cream liqueur		

Combine first 4 ingredients in a large saucepan; stir well. Cook over medium heat until thoroughly heated. Add ice cream, stirring until ice cream melts. Serve warm. Yield: 12 (1-cup) servings.

Hot Cider Punch

1	(2½-inch) stick cinnamon	8	cups apple cider
5	whole cloves	¾	cup lemon juice
10	whole allspice	¼	cup honey
2	cups orange juice	1½	teaspoons butter or margarine

Combine cinnamon stick, cloves, and allspice in a cheesecloth bag. Tie to secure.

Combine spice bag, orange juice, and remaining ingredients in a large saucepan or Dutch oven; bring to a boil. Reduce heat, cover, and simmer 1 hour; remove and discard spice bag. Yield: 8 (1-cup) servings.

Mango Bellini

1   cup diced peeled mango
      (1 medium)
2½   tablespoons fresh lime juice
6   tablespoons Sugar Syrup,
      chilled

2   cups extra-dry champagne,
      chilled
2   teaspoons grenadine syrup

Place first 3 ingredients in a food processor, and process until smooth. Strain mango purée, and discard pulp. Pour ¼ cup mango purée into each of 4 champagne glasses. Add ½ cup champagne; slowly pour ½ teaspoon grenadine down inside of each glass (do not stir before serving). Yield: 4 (¾-cup) servings.

Sugar Syrup

2   cups sugar
1   cup water

Combine sugar and water in a small saucepan; stir well. Bring mixture to a boil over medium-high heat, and cook 45 seconds or until sugar dissolves. Remove from heat; let cool. Cover and store syrup in refrigerator. Yield: 2 cups.

Recipe Index

Metric Equivalents

The recipes that appear in this cookbook use the standard United States method for measuring liquid and dry or solid ingredients (teaspoons, tablespoons, and cups). The information in the following charts is provided to help cooks outside the U.S. successfully use these recipes. All equivalents are approximate.

Equivalents for
DRY INGREDIENTS BY WEIGHT
(To convert ounces to grams,
multiply the number of ounces by 30.)

1 oz	=	1/16 lb	=	30 g
4 oz	=	1/4 lb	=	120 g
8 oz	=	1/2 lb	=	240 g
12 oz	=	3/4 lb	=	360 g
16 oz	=	1 lb	=	480 g

Equivalents for
LENGTH
(To convert inches to centimeters,
multiply the number of inches by 2.5.)

1 in				=	2.5 cm	
6 in	=	1/2 ft		=	15 cm	
12 in	=	1 ft		=	30 cm	
36 in	=	3 ft	= 1 yd	=	90 cm	
40 in				=	100 cm	= 1 m

continued on next page

Equivalents for
DIFFERENT TYPES OF INGREDIENTS

A standard cup measure of a dry or solid ingredient will vary
in weight depending on the type of ingredient. A standard cup of
liquid is the same volume for any type of liquid.
Use the following chart when converting standard cup
measures to grams (weight) or milliliters (volume).

Standard Cup	Fine Powder (ex. flour)	Grain (ex. rice)	Granular (ex. sugar)	Liquid Solids (ex. butter)	Liquid (ex. milk)
1	140 g	150 g	190 g	200 g	240 ml
¾	105 g	113 g	143 g	150 g	180 ml
⅔	93 g	100 g	125 g	133 g	160 ml
½	70 g	75 g	95 g	100 g	120 ml
⅓	47 g	50 g	63 g	67 g	80 ml
¼	35 g	38 g	48 g	50 g	60 ml
⅛	18 g	19 g	24 g	25 g	30 ml

Equivalents for
LIQUID INGREDIENTS BY VOLUME

¼ tsp			=	1 ml
½ tsp			=	2 ml
1 tsp			=	5 ml
3 tsp =	1 tbls	= ½ fl oz	=	15 ml
	2 tbls = ⅛ cup	= 1 fl oz	=	30 ml
	4 tbls = ¼ cup	= 2 fl oz	=	60 ml
	5⅓ tbls = ⅓ cup	= 3 fl oz	=	80 ml
	8 tbls = ½ cup	= 4 fl oz	=	120 ml
	10⅔ tbls = ⅔ cup	= 5 fl oz	=	160 ml
	12 tbls = ¾ cup	= 6 fl oz	=	180 ml
	16 tbls = 1 cup	= 8 fl oz	=	240 ml
	1 pt = 2 cups	= 16 fl oz	=	480 ml
	1 qt = 4 cups	= 32 fl oz	=	960 ml
		33 fl oz	=	1000 ml = 1 l

Equivalents for
COOKING/OVEN TEMPERATURES

	Fahrenheit	Celcius	Gas Mark
Freeze Water	32° F	0° C	
Room Temperature	68° F	20° C	
Boil Water	212° F	100° C	
Bake	325° F	160° C	3
	350° F	180° C	4
	375° F	190° C	5
	400° F	200° C	6
	425° F	220° C	7
	450° F	230° C	8
Broil			Grill